5

HANDBOOKS OF EUROPEAN NATIONAL DANCES

EDITED BY
VIOLET ALFORD

DANCES OF RUMANIA

Plate 1   Invârtita. Maramureş

DANCES of RUMANIA

MIRON AND CAROLA GRINDEA

PUBLISHED

UNDER THE AUSPICES OF

THE ROYAL ACADEMY OF DANCING

AND THE

LING PHYSICAL EDUCATION ASSOCIATION

A CHANTICLEER EDITION

CROWN PUBLISHERS NEW YORK

FIRST PUBLISHED IN 1952
A CHANTICLEER EDITION
CROWN PUBLISHERS
419 FOURTH AVENUE NEW YORK 16

ILLUSTRATED BY
PAMELA WOODS
ASSISTANT EDITOR
YVONNE MOYSE

SET IN 10 ON 11 POINT MONOTYPE BASKERVILLE
PRINTED BY
THE UNIVERSITY PRESS ABERDEEN SCOTLAND
PLATES IN FOUR-COLOR OFFSET-PHOTOLITHOGRAPHY

CONTENTS

Illustrations in Colour, pages 2, 12, 29, 39
Map of Rumania, page 6

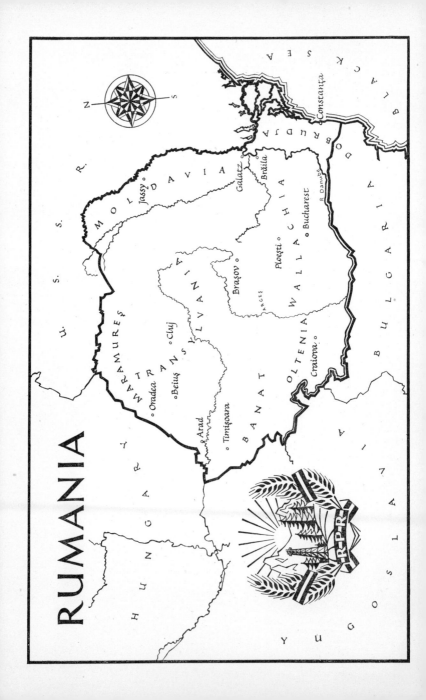

INTRODUCTION

I<small>T WAS</small> the International Folk Dance Festival held in London in the summer of 1935 which awakened attention to the pagan splendour and rhythmic subtlety of Rumanian ritual dancing. A paper read at the accompanying conference by Professor Vuia opened the eyes of the anthropological world to the extreme importance of these Spring dances. The *Times* music critic at one of the performances wrote of the 'delighted but slightly uneasy audience', wondering when, yet fearing, the thirteen Rumanian dancers would stop. According to the same paper these men 'roused the chief anthropological interest by the ritual completeness of their immense, overwhelming dance Căluşari'.

Anthropologists and historians alike have firm reasons to claim a pre-Christian antiquity for the two most characteristic Rumanian dances, the Hora and the Căluşari. It is not surprising to see a Greek origin both in name and form for the first, since many of the peoples who spread over the Carpatho-Danubian valleys—Scythians, Sarmatians and later Gauls—at least in some measure received Greek influence, brought by merchants attracted by the inexhaustible wealth of this region. The second, Căluşari, belongs to the even older class of ritual dances whose 'essential features were already developed in the tribal cultures of the Neolithic period'.*

* Curt Sachs : *World History of the Dance.* 1938.

Interest in the extraordinary features of these dances broke out afresh every time a Western traveller across the Rumanian principalities took the trouble to watch peasants on a holiday. Thus Dr. James Noyes * stressed the 'bacchic frenzy' and the harmony of these Daco-Roman 'sports'. In a still earlier account John Paget † tells us that 'the chief amusement of the Wallacks, after sleeping and smoking, is dancing to the bagpipe or fiddle. They have a custom', he writes, 'of which I never heard elsewhere. A party of idle young fellows sell themselves, as they say, to the devil for a term of three, five or seven years—the number must be unequal, or the devil will not hold the bargain—engaging to dance without ceasing during the whole of that period, except when they sleep; in consideration of which they expect their infernal purchaser will supply them with food and wine liberally, and render them irresistible among the rustic belles. Accordingly, dressed in their gayest attire, these merry vagabonds start out from their native village, and literally dance through the country. Everywhere they are received with open arms; the men glad of an excuse for jollity, the women anxious, perhaps, to prove their power, all unite to feed and fête the devil's dancers; so that it is scarcely wonderful there should be willing slaves to so merry a servitude.'

TWO THOUSAND FIVE HUNDRED DANCES

There are in fact no more than nine or ten Rumanian folk dances in living practice, but their variants and their different names, according to the various ethnical provinces, amount to the amazing number of over 2,500. This makes a thorough study of them very confusing. Though it is not easy to establish their place in popular esteem (except that of the Hora and the Sârba proper) one

* *Rumania: the Borderland of the Christian and the Turk.* 1863.
† *Hungary and Transylvania.* 1839.

can say that the best known are Bătuta, Chindia, Brâul, Ca la Breaza, Invârtita and Banul Mărăcine. As to the Căluşari, which is the most exciting and picturesque of them all, it belongs to a now disappearing category of ritual dances of which we shall speak later.

To all these, peasant dancers through the centuries have contributed hundreds of movements, postures and figures which have seemed to them to attain the widest possible degree of sociability in the most natural manner; and the fact that so many ways of skipping, hopping and stamping the earth have endured to the present day testifies to their elastic tradition and their elemental vitality. Moreover, the sturdy character of the rural Rumanians, and the fact that they make up something like 80 per cent. of the population, allows the expectation that these thousands of variants will continue to maintain their purity for many years to come.

⚜ THE HORA ⚜

There is no village in the whole country without, on a Sunday afternoon, its leaping, tightly joined chains of Hora dancers. And this applies equally to many towns where peasants have gone to work. The Hora is the most ancient, most typical and best-known of all Rumanian dances and its stimulating effect upon the community's life is perhaps without parallel in the whole of Central and South-Eastern Europe. To 'enter the Hora' means, for boys, approaching manhood, and for girls it signifies their readiness for marriage. The appeal of this age-old circular dance resides in the utter simplicity of the means it affords of meeting other people, and in its almost unique social implications. No wonder, then, that its gay character, its easy movement —anyone may join or leave the chain whenever he wishes—its somewhat indolent beauty make this dance the favourite relaxation and most endearing pastime of

9

Rumanian peasantry. A period of mourning is brought to an end by joining once more in the Hora; and, like the rigid Basque Auresku, it is used as a standard for village morals. As soon as a person of doubtful morality—an unfaithful wife, a man who has been in prison, even a youth or a girl who has broken his or her engagement—dares to enter the circle all the dancers stop at once. And there is no appeal against this collective rebuke. Townsfolk, already separated by several generations from their peasant ancestry, easily break away from their acquired snobbishness and again join in this irresistible choreographic anodyne.

The simplest form of Hora is the circle, which can start with four or five people and expand to several hundreds. Immediately after midday dinner (but preferably at dusk) young men and girls, married couples and elderly people from one or several villages will gather at the crossroads, in the barn of an inn or the courtyard of a well-to-do *gospodar* or in the vicinity of the church. A few youths whose courage and enthusiasm have been carefully stimulated by a couple of glasses of wine or plum brandy (the famous *ţuica*) are charged with the task of linking up and beginning the dance. As soon as the first circle takes shape the girls throw off their shyness and join in, then the married couples, and towards evening the over-seventies cease their endless chat to show what they too can do. And they not only stamp the ground as energetically as the rest but endow their segment of the circle with an individuality of its own.

The choreography is simple, precise, graceful and at the same time dynamic. The dancers link hands and, falling at once under the sway of the gypsy players, the circle begins to turn. One step forward, one step back, three side steps to the left, five side steps to the right, the circle thus slowly moving counter-sunwise. On they go for hours, the gypsies, *lăutari*, standing in the middle, urging, compelling, whipping on the weary, exciting the young, encouraging the old by the hypnotic power of their amazing fiddling.

This is Hora Mare, the Big Hora, everyone facing the centre, narrowing or widening the circle as the arms bend or stretch wide, surging into the centre shoulder to shoulder until they almost overwhelm the players. If the great circle seems to tire the leader will begin shouting a never-ending series of rhythmical commands, *strigături*, in sarcastic, defiant but humorous verse such as:

> *Joacă, saltă românește,*
> *Bate'n pământ voinicește,*
> *Căci țara întinerește,*
> *Pe-ai săi voinici când privește.*
>
> (Dance and leap like a Rumanian,
> Stamp the earth as it becomes you,
> For the whole country gets younger
> By merely watching its brave youngsters.)

or:

> *Cine joacă și nu strigă*
> *Facă-i-s'ar gura strâmbă.*
>
> (If you dance and do not shout
> You deserve a crooked mouth.)

—giving, as it were, more character and feeling to the ever-changing mood of the dance.

There is also a small Hora, Țărăneasca, in which only two couples take part, crossing hands behind their backs to form the circle. The left leg is advanced. One of the men then gives the signal and all four dancers turn to the right and start a series of hops ever increasing in speed. When a change of direction is needed the other man shouts '*Hai la stânga*' (Let's try the left); the four leap round to the left and continue the sunwise direction as long as they wish.

Before the last war nearly 1,600 Hora names were identifiable. Here are a few: Hora dreaptă, the Straight Hora; Hora Ielelor, the Fairies' Hora; Hora Moldovenească, Moldavian Hora; Hora Unirii, the National Union Hora—with a strong patriotic appeal; Girls' Hora; Gypsies' Hora and so forth. The word is used all over Rumania except

Plate 2   *Beiuş*

in certain Transylvanian counties, where it is called Joc Românesc, Rumanian Dance.

One of the most popular variants is Nuneasca or Hora Miresei, the Bride's Hora, which starts off outside a bride's house. This is an impressive ceremony. The bride's relations, bride and bridegroom with all their guests link hands to begin circling, using the usual steps with the addition of two stamps with the right foot. But for the best man appearing with a huge bucket of wine it might go on for ever. It is time to go to church, and even there the Hora has its place. After the priest has put the marriage wreaths on the heads of the wedded pair and administered to them the consecrated wine from the same cup, they and their parents take hands and turn about the altar in an open semicircular chain. The clergy advance singing *'Isaia dănţuieşte'* (Isaiah dances)—purifying the chain of people with clouds from the swinging censer. The altar is thus encircled three times. This typical sacred dance is to be seen at all Rumanian church marriages and can be traced back to the beginnings of the Orthodox ceremonial itself.

THE SÂRBA

Second in popularity is the Sârba. Here again we have about 300 variants of this impetuous dance. The men place their hands on their neighbours' shoulders, form a long line and dash into the 2/4 rhythm, the tempo often attaining such speed that it stupefies the dancers themselves and quite frightens the gypsy musicians who are at such pains to keep up with those they 'entertain'. A very few girls sometimes dare to join in, and when they do the curving line becomes a closed circle and the dance turns into a Hora; but usually young men only are the performers and often dance the Sârba for one hour without stopping. This chain, like the Basque Auresku and the Farandole, demands a head and a tail leader, each with his responsibilities. The head leader gives utterance to special calls meant to regulate the step and to urge on the dancers.

> *Step your steps on the same place*
> *And the Church will grow apace*

is one such rhyming command.

The chain, bow-like and hardly undulating at its centre, moves along by successive bounds to the right. Often it tightens and rolls up in a spiral. It is at this moment that the tail leader intervenes, for it is his job to lead into the 'snail' and out again, thus bringing the dancers back into their original line. This he does with astonishing precision. Both leaders never lose an opportunity of improvising new figures, after which the dance becomes a variant and is called by the name of the improviser.

It is interesting to note from a comparative, philological point of view that while Rumanians call this dance Sârba after their neighbours, the Serbs, the latter call their own version of the same dance Vlaški (from Wallachia).

Similar to the Sârba but more rapid still is the Brâul or Brâuleţul (meaning Belt), in which the dancers are linked by holding their neighbours' belts. Mocăncuţa is danced by mountaineers in couples of man and woman holding hands. Its violent exuberance which grips the partners reminds one of the Jota Aragonesa.

RITUAL DANCES

Căluşari is no doubt the oldest and most impressive among Rumanian folk dances. Owing, however, to the immense difficulties of assimilating the figures and especially to the magic atmosphere surrounding this dance—only chosen men who have gone through ascetic ordeal and submitted to strict rules of conduct are allowed to dance it—it is less widespread than the Hora or any of the dances mentioned.

A week before Whitsuntide nine men belonging to nine

neighbouring villages are selected by a leader—*vătaf* (from the Latin *vates*)—and initiated in the mystical gestures and figures of the dance. They have to wear spurred and belled boots, ribboned hats and gorgeously embroidered waistcoats. The dance proper starts before sunrise on Whitsunday. They all pray, ending with the Lord's Prayer, then each man takes the oath under the sheaths of the leader's and the dumb man's (the fool's) swords, sure that thus they will be protected against any sort of evil. Many pagan features which still adorn this elemental dance naturally differ from region to region. So, for instance, in Wallachia the men do not speak for a week while the dancing lasts. One of the men, the flag-bearer, carries a slim pole adorned with garlic and other herbs believed to have protective powers. They are constantly watched by the fairies— Ielele, Frumoasele or Rusaliile (this last word derives from the Latin Rosalia, the feast of the roses; Rusalii is also the Rumanian name for Whitsun)—so the dancers must avoid woods, waters, mounds and cross-roads where they might be caught by the fairies. According to one theory the Călușari themselves personify the fairies.

Although in a trance throughout and although the dancing lasts for hours without a break, the men leap on, leaning on their sticks and never holding hands; this is thought to be the way goddesses would dance. But the very fact that after the dance is over they destroy all their insignia and dance ornaments, such as hare-skin, sticks and whips, and run away without looking back indicates that the Călușari do fear the fairies. At any rate there is no doubt about the popular belief in their healing attributes and the curative effect of their dancing. Young women and girls always try to dance near the Călușari in order to remain healthy and attractive; children are thrown into their arms in the hope they will grow big and strong, while many variants of the Călușari undertake the healing even of grown-ups, leaping over a sick person laid on the ground in their path.

Many customs like the destruction or burial of all attributes, the blacking of the face, the uneven number and the exclusively men dancers, and especially the connections with the fairies and the sun made in most of the regions where this dance is still cultivated point to the fact that the Călușari are among the most valuable remnants of prehistoric rites. The dance is a wonder in itself and its mythological implications will continue to preoccupy anthropologists for a long time to come. In Dimitrie Cantemir's famous *Descriptio Moldaviae*, published in the eighteenth century, we are told that the Călușari 'wear feminine costumes, speak like women, put wreaths of flowers on their heads and disguise their faces with white veils, each one having a naked sword in his hand'. Curt Sachs, however, insists that 'the uneven number prescribed for the participants and for the years they pledge themselves to dance points to the masculine culture'.

There are many other ritual, fertility, ghost, work, game, and healing dances although none reaches the splendour of the Călușari. The most important is Capra (The Goat), which is performed with pomp and circumstance on New Year's Eve when fresh hopes arise for the coming year. Men, dressed up as animals, sing and dance before villagers' houses, one disguised as a goat. (In certain parts of Transylvania he appears as a stag.) Gifts are made to the dancers and a different wish is uttered in exchange for each gift. The man who plays the part of the goat is supposed to personify the Devil and cannot therefore enter any church for seven years. Other characters are the Chief or Imperator, the mare which carries the bag for presents, three cats and other animals. Sometimes the goat has a stork-beak, linking him with the beaked masks of Austria and Switzerland. In Wallachia the group of dancers stop passers-by and start a Hora round them; if they do not receive enough money or presents the goat howls dismally and the Hora goes on and on round the mean person.

The Vicleim, or Bethleem, or Irozii (from Irod, i.e. Herod, Governor of Judea, one of the main characters in the play), is a religious drama celebrating the birth of Christ interspersed with dances of a solemn character. In Wallachia the king is accompanied by a fool, an officer and fifteen boys as counsellors, while in Moldavia there appear two angels, shepherds and many servants. As the ceremony lasts a long time and as the *mise-en-scène* is quite expensive, no more than two or three performances by the same troupe can take place on Christmas Eve and the following nights, so that the whole village follows the actors to gaze their fill. Often one team of performers will visit some fifty villages.

Plugușorul is a little plough decorated with coloured papers and artificial flowers, pulled by young boys who recite short ballads and plough furrows in the peasants' yards. The recitations are interrupted by dancing steps, cracking whips and by the throwing of handfuls of seeds. The verses are constantly accompanied by the noise produced by a horsehair string pulled through the leather cover of a barrel. This produces strange vibrations said to imitate the bellowing of a bull; hence the instrument is called *buhaiu*, which means bull.

Without going into further details one can safely say that owing to Rumanian peasant life having remained traditionally patriarchal, research into all these forms of artistic culture still rewards the student and yields most interesting results.

MUSIC

Rumanian folk music is as ancient, varied and expressive as the country's folk dances. Foreign chroniclers and travellers speak of the melancholy beauty of Rumania's popular songs and the richness of the rhythms, and all stress in particular the historical heritage of the Thracians. Some of the instruments have been in use for over two thousand years, having been inherited from the Western Roman Empire. One of these is the *buciumul* (Lat. *buccina*), a large tube-like instrument, 3 to 9 ft. in length, slightly curved and made of the bark of the lime-tree bound round with cherry-tree bark. This is still used by shepherds. One also comes across many types of flutes ; the *caval*, with a beautiful sound, the *tilinca*, without stops and made of maple bark, lime bark or osier, and the very popular *fluier*, a primitive pipe. The *naiu* is a more elaborate instrument with a powerful tone, made of several flutes put together.

One can hardly imagine dancing without a band worthy of the occasion. The most frequent ensemble consists of a fiddle supported by a *cobza* (a type of lute made of maple wood with ten to fifteen strings). The players are usually gypsies, born musicians with an astonishing sense of rhythm but who, unfortunately, never can resist the temptation to alter tunes, to adapt them to suit their fancy or the mood displayed in the dance. There is hardly a big Hora when the musicians will not improvise a new tune; the improvisation is accompanied by satirical jokes, music and words engendered by the excitement of the dance. In Transylvania and many other parts of the country the *cobza* is replaced by the *ţambal*, a cimbalom with wooden box and metal strings which the player hits with two small hammers. The trumpet and clarinet are also used though less frequently. George Enesco's famous Rumanian Rhapsody in A major has popularised the most characteristic effects obtained by these blends of popular instruments and rhythmical patterns.

⁂ COSTUME ⁂

Rumanian peasant folk possess even greater wealth in their marvellous diversity of costume than in their melodies and rhythms. Since the folk dances have a distinct social significance it is natural that costume should play an important role in all dance occasions. Traditional costumes bear the imprint of geographical and climatic conditions as well as that of the regional peasant art. A most important and interesting fact is the undoubted descent of many costumes and parts of costumes still worn today from the dress of the Daco-Roman ancestors. Indeed on the Trajan Column in Rome one can pick out the exact image of many costumes still found in Rumania today.

Although men's dress varies from one province to another in details, fundamentally it presents the same characteristics almost everywhere: very tight white breeches, *iţari*, a white shirt richly festooned, generally in black and white, round the neck and sleeves and at the hem. This shirt is slightly gathered in round the waist by a hand-woven belt of most ingenious design and colouring, in which red predominates. Waistcoats are usually of white hand-woven wool, lavishly embroidered, or of sheepskin with the wool inside. Hats are often adorned with feathers or natural flowers, and fur caps appear in the winter.

Women's costumes are more complicated and varied. The blouses have round necks and very wide sleeves gathered at the wrists, with embroidery in silk from their own silkworms. Into the designs women and girls put all their imagination and hopes, creating exquisite and intricate patterns. With these blouses very full skirts are worn. In Moldavia, over the skirts women wear a *catrinţa*, a large piece of wool in many colours, tight over the hips, tied on the left side, while the bottom corner is turned up and pinned in place. In other regions of the country women wear *fote*, a sort of double apron, which is in two panels, one in front, the other at the back.

The *maramă*, head-kerchief, is an important item, each province showing its own characteristics. Married women tie theirs under the chin, leaving no hair visible; girls wear theirs in a great variety of ways.

THE DANCES

TECHNICAL EDITORS
MURIEL WEBSTER AND KATHLEEN P. TUCK

༚༺༻༚

ABBREVIATIONS
USED IN DESCRIPTION OF STEPS AND DANCES

r—right⎫ referring to
l— left ⎭ hand, foot, etc.

C—clockwise

R—right⎫ describing turns or
L—left ⎭ ground pattern

C-C—counter-clockwise

For descriptions of foot positions and explanations of any ballet terms the following books are suggested for reference:

A Primer of Classical Ballet (Cecchetti method). Cyril Beaumont.

First Steps (R.A.D.). Ruth French and Felix Demery.

The Ballet Lover's Pocket Book. Kay Ambrose.

POISE OF BODY AND HOLDS

The poise is generally dignified and upright, even majestic; becoming less so in the excitement of the dance (see Sârba, Plate 3). The woman's movements are quieter and her steps lower than the man's.

The following holds are used:—

1. Hands on hips: the thumbs are backward and the fingers forward.

2. Arms folded: for men—see Banul Mărăcine.

3. Shoulder grasp:
   (*a*) In lines.
   (*b*) Partners facing each other.

4. Waist-and-shoulder grasp: Partners stand facing one another, the man grasping his partner by the waist while she has her hands on his shoulders.

5. Hand grasp: Partners grasp r hand with r hand or vice versa, with the hands held about shoulder height.

BASIC STEPS

Change-of-Step Hop
Step forward on r foot.
Close l foot behind.
Step forward on r foot and hop on r, with l knee raised forward.

Step-Hop
This can be taken with either a hop or a lilt, according to the tempo of the music and mood of the dance.

Spurs
This is a form of cabriole danced as follows:
Hop on one foot with other leg lifted sideways.
Click heels together, bringing lifted leg towards hopping foot.
The lift of the leg is a preparation, and the click of the heels comes *on* the beat. These may be 2 or 4 to a bar; see Banul Mărăcine.

Step and Throw (Invârtita)	*Beats*
Step to side on r foot.	1
Close l foot behind r foot.	and
Step on to r foot and throw l foot across in front.	2

SÂRBA

Region   All over the country. (Plate 3.)

Character   Quick and energetic; danced chiefly by men. They use a shoulder grasp, and the two leaders have their free hand on the hip.

Formation   A line, or a circle which is not closed. There is the first leader, a reliable dancer, at the head of the line, and a second at the end of the line.

Dance

There is only one step.

Step to R on r foot and hop on the r foot, with the l knee bent up in front. Repeat this to L with l foot.

I

SÂRBA

Allegro con fuoco ($\flat$ = 108-112)

Arranged by Arnold Foster

Step to R with r foot; close l foot behind r; step on to r foot and hop, swinging l leg across with knee slightly bent. || 2

Step to L with l foot and hop on the l foot, with the r knee bent up in front. || 3 (beat 1)

Moving to the R, take Change-of-step (r, close, r). || (beat 2)

Hop on r foot, with l knee raised in front. || 4 (beat 1)

(The whole of this part takes $3\frac{1}{2}$ bars of music.) ||

N.B.—The dance must be started with a step and hop on the r foot, then on the l, followed by a Change-of-step hop on the r foot. After this the dance goes on with the Step-hop only on the l foot and the Change-of-step hop on the r foot, as in Bar 3 and beat 1 of Bar 4. This step, which takes $1\frac{1}{2}$ bars of music, is repeated until the dance is finished, and the music (bars 1–18, with repeats) is played as often as desired.

The first leader must keep the dance in a line or circle, helped in this by the second leader.

Region   All parts of Rumania.

Character   The easiest and most popular of Rumanian folk dances, with smooth, swaying movements.

Formation   Circle dance for any number of dancers from four only to several hundred. The hands are joined and held shoulder-high.

Dance	MUSIC *Bars*
FIGURE I	
Lilt forward on r foot, with l leg raised behind with the knee slightly bent. Lilt backward on l foot, with r leg raised in front with the knee slightly bent.	1
3 steps forward—r [*beat 1*], l [*and*], r [*beat 2*]—closing the circle.	2
Repeat the movements of bars 1 and 2 but lilt backward on to l foot first, and open the circle on the 3 walks.	3–4
Repeat the movements of bars 1–4.	5–8
FIGURE II: THE BALANCE	
Step sideways on r foot and lilt, swinging the l leg across with the knee slightly bent. Repeat this, stepping on to l foot.	9
Moving to the R, step r foot [*beat 1*]; cross l foot behind r [*and*]; step sideways again with r foot [*beat 2*].	10
Repeat the movements of bars 9–10, moving to the L and stepping on to l foot.	11–12

HORA

Arranged by Arnold Foster

Repeat the movements of bars 9–12.   13–16

FIGURE III

8 lilting skips moving C-C, starting with r foot.   17–20
The first two are taken with the back to the
line of dance (i.e. moving C-C, with body
and feet turned to face C). The next two
skips are taken facing the line of dance.

Repeat the movements of bars 17–20 in the   21–24
same way but move C.

The dance can be repeated as often as the
dancers wish.

BANUL MĂRĂCINE

Region   Very popular in Moldavia, Wallachia, Oltenia and Dobrudja.

Character   A dignified, even majestic dance.

Formation   Any number of dancers, or a solo. If by two, they stand facing one another, the man with arms folded in front, the woman with hands on hips. If several dancers, they stand in a line or semicircle with shoulder grasp.

Dance	MUSIC *Bars*
FIGURE I	A
Hop on l, pointing r foot in front and across l foot. Hop on l, pointing r foot across behind l foot.	I
3 light stamps [*beats 1–3*]. Hold [*beat 4*].	2
Repeat movements of bar 1 with opposite foot.	3
'Conclusion'—Hop on r, pointing l foot in front and across r foot [*beat 1*]. Hop on r foot, pointing l foot sideways [*beat 2*]. Spring feet together [*beat 3*]. Hold [*beat 4*].	4
FIGURE II	
Hop on l foot while pointing r foot on the toe, then the heel, in 2nd position [*beats 1–2*]. Repeat [*beats 3–4*].	I
Repeat movements of bar 1 with other foot.	2
Repeat movements of bar 1.	3
'Conclusion' with l foot.	4

Plate 3   Sârba. Dragoş village, Transylvania

FIGURE III
B

Hop on l, pointing r foot forward on toe; hop
again on l foot, with r leg raised forward with
a slightly bent knee.

5

Spring with feet together, making a quarter-
turn to the L; then hop on l foot, lifting r leg
backward with a slightly bent knee.

6

Repeat movements of bars 5–6, hopping on
r and pointing l foot, taking a quarter-turn
back to R while springing feet together.

7–8

Repeat movements of bar 5 twice.

9–10

'Conclusion' with l foot.

11–12

BANUL MĂRĂCINE

Arranged by Arnold Foster

30

Play AA, BB, CC, DD, EE, AA.

FIGURE IV: SPURS (TWICE)

Moving sideways to R, hop twice on l foot, clicking the heels together (in the air).   5–6

3 stamps in place—r, l, r; hold.   7–8

Repeat movements of bars 5–6, moving to L and hopping on r foot.   9–10

'Conclusion' with l foot.   11–12

FIGURE V: SPURS (FOUR TIMES)   C

As in Figure IV, but clicking the heels more quickly and 4 times.   13

3 stamps in place—r, l, r; hold.   14

As in bar 13, but hop on r foot.   15

'Conclusion' with l foot.   16

FIGURE VI: KNEELING

With a spring make a quarter-turn to the R, kneeling on l knee, with r bent up in front [*beat 1*]. Hold [*beat 2*]. Spring to face forward again with feet together [*beat 3*]. Hold [*beat 4*].   13

3 stamps in place—r, l, r.   14

Repeat as in bar 13, turning to L, on opposite knee. Spring to face forward, feet together.   15

'Conclusion' with l foot.   16

FIGURE VII: RESTING   D

With a small spring cross the feet so that the l is in front, and stand still in this position on the toes, with the l hand on the hip and the r holding the back of the head.   17

3 stamps—r, l, r—with hands on hips.   18

As in bar 17, but with r foot across and with l hand holding the back of the head.   19

'Conclusion' with l foot, bringing hands to hips.   20

FIGURE VIII

> With a quarter-turn to the R, jump with feet together, followed by 2 runs on the spot—r, l —lifting the feet quickly backward. 17
> 3 stamps—r, l, r. 18
> Repeat as in bar 17, making a quarter-turn back to L with 2 turns—l, r. 19
> 'Conclusion' with l foot. 20

E

FIGURE IX

> With a small spring cross the feet so that the l foot is in front. Repeat, changing the feet. 21
> 3 stamps—r, l, r. 22
> Repeat as in bar 21, crossing r foot in front. 23
> 'Conclusion' with l foot. 24

FIGURE X

> Quarter-turn to R with 2 hops—l, r. 21
> With a quarter-turn to L, 'Conclusion' with l foot. 22
> Quarter-turn to L with 2 hops—r, l. 23
> With a quarter-turn to R, 'Conclusion' with r foot. 24

A

FIGURE XI

> Spring to cross the feet, with r foot in front, and clap the hands behind the back [*beat 1*]. Hold [*beat 2*]. Hop on the l foot, lifting the r leg forward with the knee bent, and clap under the raised knee [*beat 3*]. Hold [*beat 4*]. 1
> 3 stamps—r, l, r. 2
> As in bar 1, with l foot. 3
> 'Conclusion' with l foot. 4

FIGURE XII

> Dancers retire by taking small neat skipping steps backward, starting with r foot. 1–4

INVÂRTITA

Ana Lugojana

❋❋❋❋❋❋

Region   Introduced from Transylvania and the Banat into the rest of the country. (Plate 1.)

Character   A gay, quick dance which is an adaptation of the Polka.

Formation   Couple dance. Dancers stand side by side in a semicircle, with inside hands on partner's shoulder and outside hands on the hip.

Dance	MUSIC
	Bars
FIGURE I	A
a Step and throw r foot.	1
Repeat this on l foot.	2
Repeat movements of bars 1–2.	3–4
b Partners face with waist-and-shoulder grasp. They turn together C with 6 quick runs followed by 1 Step-hop.	5–6
Repeat movements of bars 5–6 but turn C-C.	7–8
FIGURE II	
a As in Figure I*a*.	1–4
b Partners link r arms and turn together C on the spot with 6 runs followed by 1 Step-hop.	5–6
Repeat movements of bars 5–6 with l arms linked and turning C-C.	7–8

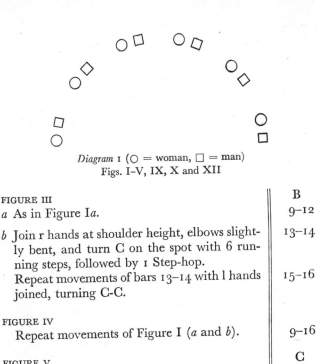

Diagram 1 (○ = woman, □ = man)
Figs. I–V, IX, X and XII

FIGURE III	**B**
a As in Figure I*a*.	9–12
b Join r hands at shoulder height, elbows slightly bent, and turn C on the spot with 6 running steps, followed by 1 Step-hop.	13–14
Repeat movements of bars 13–14 with l hands joined, turning C-C.	15–16
FIGURE IV	
Repeat movements of Figure I (*a* and *b*).	9–16
FIGURE V	**C**
a As in Figure I*a*.	17–20
b Partners face with waist-and-shoulder grasp. They turn on the spot to the man's R with 4 very quick steps—r, l, r, and hop on r foot.	17
Repeat these movements to L, starting l foot.	18
Repeat movements of bars 17–18.	19–20
FIGURE VI	**D**
a As in Figure I*a*.	21–24
b THE GALLOP	**E**
In this the couples change places and move from the semicircle into two lines facing one	

INVÂRTITA: ANA LUGOJANA

Arranged by Arnold Foster

Allegro con brio

GALLOP
Tempo primo

Play **AA, BB, CC, D, EE** *twice through; finish with* **AA.**

another, each woman standing on the R of her
partner. To do this, the couples on one side
of the semicircle start with the r foot and
those on the other side with the l foot.

Couples on R gallop sideways to L for 4 steps.	25–26
Place r foot across in front of l foot, with toe pointed, and hold this position.	27–28

N.B.—Couples on L will do the same but with
the opposite foot, and move to the R.

Repeat movements of bars 25–28, moving in opposite direction with smaller steps.	29–32
Repeat movements of bars 25–32; end in two lines facing, with partners side by side.	25–32

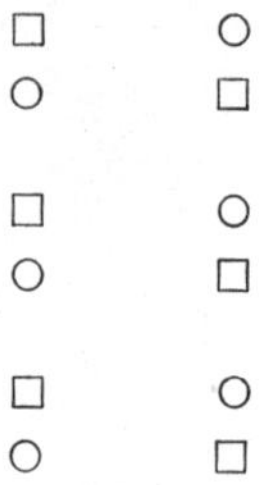

□　　○　　　　　□ ←○　　○→ □
○　　□

□　　○　　　　　□ ←○　　○→ □
○　　□

□　　○　　　　　□ ←○　　○→ □
○　　□

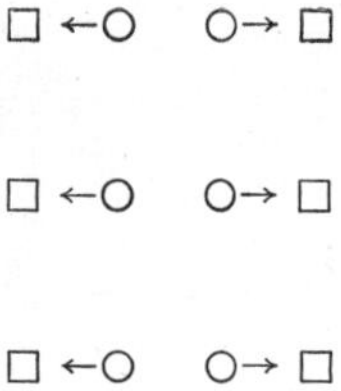

Diagram 3
Figs. VII and VIII
re-forming semicircle
as in Fig. I

Diagram 2
Gallop: Figs. VI*b* and XI

FIGURE VII	**A**
a As in Figure I*a*.	1–4
b Each woman turns under her partner's r arm with 4 walking steps, to end facing him on the 4th beat.	5–6
Partners bow to one another.	7–8
Women stand still with hands on hips to watch the men, who dance the steps of Figure I*a* twice.	1–8
FIGURE VIII	**B**
4 walking steps, man moving forward to lead his partner who moves backward.	9–10
Repeat, but man backward to pull his partner forward.	11–12
Repeat movements of bars 1–4 but end having made a quarter-turn to the R.	13–16
Repeat movements of bars 9–16 but end in semicircle as in start of dance, with inside hands shoulder grasp, outside hands on hips.	9–16
FIGURE IX	**C**
As in Figure V (*a* and *b*).	17–20 twice

38

Plate 4   Argeş

FIGURE X	D
As in Figure I*a*.	21–24
FIGURE XI: THE GALLOP	E
As in Figure VI*b*.	25–32
	twice
FIGURE XII	A
a As in Figure I*a*.	1–4
b Partners change places with 4 walking steps.	5–6
Bow to one another.	7–8
Change places again with 4 walking steps.	1–2
Bow to one another.	3–4
All bow to dancer standing on R.	5–6
All bow to dancer on L.	7–8

BIBLIOGRAPHY

BARTÓK, BÉLA.—*La Musique populaire des Hongrois et des peuples voisins.* Budapest, 1936. (*Archivum Europae Centro-Orientalis,* tom. 2, fasc. 3–4.)

BRUN, JULES.—*Les Noces valaques.* (*Le Vieux pays roumain.*) Paris, 1891.

DÉMIDOFF, ANATOLE DE.—*Voyage dans la Russie méridionale et la Crimée par la Hongrie, la Valachie et la Moldavie.* 4 vols. Paris, 1840–42.

PAMFILE, TUDOR.—*Sărbători de vară la Români.* Bucharest, 1913. (Rumanian Summer Feasts.)

PÂRVAN, VASILE.—*Dacia: an outline of the early civilizations of the Carpatho-Danubian countries.* Cambridge, 1928.

PÂRVESCU, POMPILIU.—*Hora din Cartal.* Bucharest, 1908. (*Biblioteca Academiei Române.*) (The Hora of Cartal.)

UBICINI, M.—*Valachie, Moldavie, Bukovine, Transylvanie, Bessarabie.* Paris, 1856.

VUIA, ROMUL.—'Originea jocului de Călușari.' *Dacoromania* (Cluj), 1921. (The Origin of the Călușari Dance.)

—— 'The Rumanian Hobby-Horse, the Călușari.' *Journal of the English Folk Dance and Song Society,* vol. II, 1935.

VULPESCU, MIHAIL.—*Cântecul popular românesc.* Bucharest, 1930. (Rumanian Folk Song.)

C 49¢